Things Emotions Are Allowed to Do

(An Incomplete List)

About This Book

This is an incomplete list.

Emotions are not problems to be solved or eliminated. They are part of being human. This book offers examples of what different emotions are allowed to do—but it does not attempt to name or define every feeling.

There is no complete list.

You are invited to add to it.

There is no right way to draw or describe your feelings. What you notice and how you express it belongs to you.

Emotions We Will Learn About

Happy, Ecstatic, Confident, Mischievous, Lovestruck
Giddy, Surprised, Smug, Confused, Suspicious
Cautious, Shy, Embarrassed, Guilty, Ashamed
Bored, Lonely, Sad, Depressed, Exhausted
Frustrated, Anxious, Overwhelmed, Frightened, Shocked
Disgusted, Jealous, Angry, Enraged, Relieved, Hopeful

For each emotion we will learn what they mean and how they are expressed in a healthy way.

There is plenty of space to write and draw to express the feeling in your own way. You can draw faces, colors, shapes, or moments—there is no right way.

Your art is for you and if you want to talk to an adult about a strong emotion you have about something, you can look for a safe adult to open up to.

Table of Contents

Navigating Your Feelings

Happy

Happy is allowed to show on your face.
Happy is allowed to make you want to dance.
Happy is allowed to be loud.
Happy is allowed to make you want to hug someone (but ask first).
Happy is allowed to show up for no reason at all.
Happy is allowed to be quiet too — like a warm feeling in your chest that only you know about.

Can you think of a time you felt this way?
Draw it or write about it.

Ecstatic

Ecstatic is allowed to be bigger than happy.
Ecstatic is allowed to make you jump up and down.
Ecstatic is allowed to come out as a scream.
Ecstatic is allowed to make you cry happy tears.
Ecstatic is allowed to feel like you might burst.
Ecstatic is allowed to be hard to explain — sometimes the biggest feelings don't have enough words.

Can you think of a time you felt this way?
Draw it or write about it.

Confident

Confident is allowed to stand up straight.
Confident is allowed to raise your hand even when you're not 100% sure.
Confident is allowed to say "I've got this."
Confident is allowed to take up space.
Confident is allowed to look someone in the eye.
Confident is allowed to feel different from bragging — confident is about you, not about being better than someone else.

Can you think of a time you felt this way?
Draw it or write about it.

Mischievous

Mischievous is allowed to make you smile a sneaky little smile.
Mischievous is allowed to come up with silly ideas.
Mischievous is allowed to make you giggle before the joke even lands.
Mischievous is allowed to be playful.
Mischievous is allowed to know the difference between a prank that makes everyone laugh and one that only makes you laugh.

Can you think of a time you felt this way?
Draw it or write about it.

Lovestruck

Lovestruck is allowed to make your heart feel fluttery.
Lovestruck is allowed to make you want to be near someone all the time.
Lovestruck is allowed to make you a little silly.
Lovestruck is allowed to be about a person, a pet, or even a place.
Lovestruck is allowed to make you nervous and happy at the same time.
Lovestruck is allowed to stay just in your heart — you don't have to tell anyone if you're not ready.

Can you think of a time you felt this way?
Draw it or write about it.

Giddy

Giddy is allowed to make you laugh until your stomach hurts.
Giddy is allowed to make you laugh until you cry.
Giddy is allowed to be contagious — sometimes you don't even know what's funny anymore.
Giddy is allowed to show up at unexpected times.
Giddy is allowed to feel like too much and just right at the same time.
Giddy is allowed to need a moment to calm down — and that's okay too.

Can you think of a time you felt this way?
Draw it or write about it.

Surprised

Surprised is allowed to make your eyes go wide.
Surprised is allowed to make you gasp.
Surprised is allowed to be happy or uncomfortable — not all surprises feel the same.
Surprised is allowed to need a second to catch up with what just happened.
Surprised is allowed to make you laugh, or freeze, or even cry.
Surprised is allowed to remind you that you don't have to have everything figured out ahead of time.

Can you think of a time you felt this way?
Draw it or write about it.

Smug

Smug is allowed to show up when you were right about something.
Smug is allowed to feel satisfying for a moment.
Smug is allowed to be honest — sometimes winning feels good.
Smug is allowed to be what happens when confidence gets a little too big for its britches.
Smug is allowed to be what pride looks like when it stops paying attention to other people.
Smug is allowed to step aside for humility.

Can you think of a time you felt this way?
Draw it or write about it.

Confused

Confused is allowed to make you stop and scratch your head.
Confused is allowed to ask questions — as many as you need.
Confused is allowed to feel uncomfortable when everyone else seems to understand and you don't.
Confused is allowed to be the beginning of learning something new.
Confused is allowed to say "I don't know" out loud.
Confused is allowed to be okay with not having all the answers yet.

Can you think of a time you felt this way?
Draw it or write about it.

Suspicious

Suspicious is allowed to make you slow down before you trust something.
Suspicious is allowed to ask "does this seem right to me?"
Suspicious is allowed to be your brain trying to keep you safe.
Suspicious is allowed to pay attention to that funny feeling in your stomach.
Suspicious is allowed to say "I need more information before I decide."
Suspicious is allowed to be one of the ways you learn to trust your own instincts.

Can you think of a time you felt this way?
Draw it or write about it.

Cautious

Cautious is allowed to make you look both ways twice.
Cautious is allowed to slow down when everyone else is rushing.
Cautious is allowed to say "let me think about this first."
Cautious is allowed to feel like the difference between a good idea and a really good idea.
Cautious is allowed to be mistaken for fear — but cautious is fear that learned how to think.
Cautious is allowed to be one of the bravest things you can be.

Can you think of a time you felt this way?
Draw it or write about it.

Shy

Shy is allowed to make you want to stay close to someone you trust.
Shy is allowed to take a little longer to warm up to new people.
Shy is allowed to be quiet in a room full of loud.
Shy is allowed to watch before you jump in.
Shy is allowed to be mistaken for unfriendly — but shy just needs a little more time.
Shy is allowed to come out of hiding when it feels safe.

Can you think of a time you felt this way?
Draw it or write about it.

Embarrassed

Embarrassed is allowed to make your face turn red.
Embarrassed is allowed to make you want to disappear for a minute.
Embarrassed is allowed to show up even when you didn't do anything wrong.
Embarrassed is allowed to feel bigger in the moment than it really is.
Embarrassed is allowed to be survived — almost everyone in the room has felt it too.
Embarrassed is allowed to become a funny story later.

Can you think of a time you felt this way?
Draw it or write about it.

Guilty

Guilty is allowed to feel heavy.
Guilty is allowed to be your heart telling you that something matters.
Guilty is allowed to make you want to make things right.
Guilty is allowed to point you toward an apology.
Guilty is allowed to be proof that you have a conscience — and that's a good thing to have.
Guilty is allowed to leave once you've made it right.

Can you think of a time you felt this way?
Draw it or write about it.

Ashamed

Ashamed is allowed to feel even heavier than guilty.
Ashamed is allowed to make you want to hide.
Ashamed is allowed to be the difference between "I did something bad" and "I am bad" — and that difference matters.
Ashamed is allowed to be wrong about you.
Ashamed is allowed to need someone safe to talk to.
Ashamed is allowed to leave — you are not the worst thing you ever did.

Can you think of a time you felt this way?
You don't have to draw or write about this one. But if you want to, here's some space.

Bored

Bored is allowed to make everything feel slow and flat.
Bored is allowed to be uncomfortable — it doesn't have to be fixed right away.
Bored is allowed to be the empty space where a good idea is about to grow.
Bored is allowed to make you restless.
Bored is allowed to be a sign that you are ready for something new.
Bored is allowed to teach you how to be alone with yourself.

Can you think of a time you felt this way?
Draw it or write about it.

Lonely

Lonely is allowed to show up even in a room full of people.
Lonely is allowed to make you ache for someone who understands.
Lonely is allowed to be different from being alone — you can be alone and perfectly happy, and you can be lonely in a crowd.
Lonely is allowed to make you reach out to someone.
Lonely is allowed to remind you that connection matters to you — and that's not a weakness.
Lonely is allowed to lead you toward the people who are right for you.

Can you think of a time you felt this way?
Draw it or write about it.

Sad

Sad is allowed to make you cry.
Sad is allowed to need a blanket and a quiet place.
Sad is allowed to show up without a reason big enough to explain it.
Sad is allowed to be felt all the way through instead of pushed down.
Sad is allowed to make you want someone to sit with you — even if neither of you says a word.
Sad is allowed to pass — not because you forced it, but because you let it move through you.

Can you think of a time you felt this way?
Draw it or write about it.

Depressed

Depressed is allowed to feel like sad's heavier, longer cousin.
Depressed is allowed to show up even when you can't point to one clear reason.
Depressed is allowed to stick around longer than you want it to.
Depressed is allowed to make everything feel gray.
Depressed is allowed to make even small things feel heavy.
Depressed is allowed to make it hard to explain what's wrong — sometimes there aren't enough words.
Depressed is allowed to need help figuring out what's going on.
Depressed is allowed to need more than a blanket and a quiet place — sometimes it needs a grownup or someone safe who can help.
Depressed is allowed to be taken seriously.

Can you think of a time you felt this way?
You don't have to draw or write about this one. But if you want to, here's some space.

Exhausted

Exhausted is allowed to make your body feel like it weighs a thousand pounds.
Exhausted is allowed to show up after something hard — or after something wonderful.
Exhausted is allowed to need more than one good night of sleep.
Exhausted is allowed to say "I have nothing left right now."
Exhausted is allowed to be a signal that you have been giving a lot of yourself.
Exhausted is allowed to rest without feeling guilty about it.

Can you think of a time you felt this way?
Draw it or write about it.

Frustrated

Frustrated is allowed to make you want to scrunch up your whole face.
Frustrated is allowed to show up when you keep trying and it keeps not working.
Frustrated is allowed to make you need to take a break and come back.
Frustrated is allowed to be proof that you care about getting it right.
Frustrated is allowed to stomp around a little — as long as nobody gets hurt.
Frustrated is allowed to be the feeling right before you figure it out.

Can you think of a time you felt this way?
Draw it or write about it.

Anxious

Anxious is allowed to make your stomach feel like it's full of butterflies that forgot how to fly.
Anxious is allowed to ask "what if" a hundred times in a row.
Anxious is allowed to show up even when everything is actually okay.
Anxious is allowed to make you want to avoid the thing that scares you — but it's allowed to be wrong about that plan.
Anxious is allowed to need someone to help you think through what's real and what's worry.
Anxious is allowed to get smaller when you walk toward it instead of away from it.

Can you think of a time you felt this way?
Draw it or write about it.

Overwhelmed

Overwhelmed is allowed to make you feel like there is too much of everything all at once.
Overwhelmed is allowed to make it hard to know where to start.
Overwhelmed is allowed to need everything to get a little quieter for a minute.
Overwhelmed is allowed to ask for help sorting out what matters most right now.
Overwhelmed is allowed to do just one small thing — and let that be enough for today.
Overwhelmed is allowed to remind you that you are only one person, and that is okay.

Can you think of a time you felt this way?
Draw it or write about it.

Frightened

Frightened is allowed to make your heart pound loud and fast.
Frightened is allowed to make you want to run or freeze right where you are.
Frightened is allowed to be your body trying to protect you.
Frightened is allowed to need a safe person right away.
Frightened is allowed to be taken seriously — even if the thing that scared you seems small to someone else.
Frightened is allowed to get smaller when someone you trust is close by.

Can you think of a time you felt this way?
You don't have to draw or write about this one. But if you want to, here's some space.

Shocked

Shocked is allowed to stop you completely in your tracks.
Shocked is allowed to make your mouth fall open and your brain go quiet.
Shocked is allowed to need a minute before you know how you feel about what just happened.
Shocked is allowed to be the moment between something happening and your feelings catching up.
Shocked is allowed to turn into something else once it settles — sadness, relief, anger, or joy.
Shocked is allowed to remind you that some things in life you simply cannot see coming.

Can you think of a time you felt this way?
Draw it or write about it.

Disgusted

Disgusted is allowed to make your face scrunch up and your stomach turn.
Disgusted is allowed to say "no thank you" to something that doesn't feel right.
Disgusted is allowed to be about a smell, a taste, or something you saw.
Disgusted is allowed to be about something unfair or unkind — not everything that disgusts us is on a plate.
Disgusted is allowed to have good instincts — sometimes disgusted is pointing at something worth paying attention to.
Disgusted is allowed to move you to do something about what you see.

Can you think of a time you felt this way?
Draw it or write about it.

Jealous

Jealous is allowed to show up when someone has something you wish you had.
Jealous is allowed to be honest — wanting good things for yourself is not wrong.
Jealous is allowed to tell you something about what you care about.
Jealous is allowed to be the beginning of a conversation with yourself about what you really want.
Jealous is allowed to notice when it has crossed into wanting to take something away from someone else — that's when it needs to stop and think.
Jealous is allowed to turn into motivation instead of meanness.

Can you think of a time you felt this way?
Draw it or write about it.

Angry

Angry is allowed to make your face get hot and your fists want to clench.
Angry is allowed to be loud — with your words, not your hands.
Angry is allowed to say "that was not okay."
Angry is allowed to be about something that really matters.
Angry is allowed to be felt all the way through — but your hands are allowed to stay to yourself while you feel it.
Angry is allowed to be the feeling that tells you something needs to change.

Can you think of a time you felt this way?
Draw it or write about it.

Enraged

Enraged is allowed to feel like angry turned up all the way.
Enraged is allowed to feel like too much to hold inside.
Enraged is allowed to need space — away from other people until it cools down.
Enraged is allowed to need your body to move — run, jump, shake it out.
Enraged is allowed to not be in charge of your words or your hands — which is exactly why it needs space first.
Enraged is allowed to cool down into something you can actually work with.

Can you think of a time you felt this way?
Draw it or write about it.

Relieved

Relieved is allowed to feel like putting down something heavy you didn't realize you were carrying.
Relieved is allowed to make you exhale all the way.
Relieved is allowed to make you laugh and cry at the same time.
Relieved is allowed to show up after something hard is finally over.
Relieved is allowed to remind you how much you were holding on — and how strong you were to hold it.
Relieved is allowed to make room for what comes next.

Can you think of a time you felt this way?
Draw it or write about it.

Hopeful

Hopeful is allowed to show up even after the hardest days.
Hopeful is allowed to be small at first — just a tiny light at the end of a long hallway.
Hopeful is allowed to not have all the details figured out yet.
Hopeful is allowed to believe that things can get better without knowing exactly how.
Hopeful is allowed to be the bravest feeling of all — because it keeps going anyway.
Hopeful is allowed to be yours — no matter what.

Can you think of a time you felt this way?
Draw it or write about it.

What emotions would you add to this list?

A Note for When You've Had a Big Moment

Maybe you screamed into a pillow. Maybe you ran around the block three times as fast as you could. Maybe you cried so hard you couldn't breathe, or said something out loud that surprised even you.

That's okay.

Safe adults are not keeping a list of everything you did when your feelings got very big. They are not waiting to judge you for it. They are not embarrassed by you.

They are just waiting.

Waiting to sit with you. Waiting to hear about it when you're ready. Waiting to help you figure out what was underneath all of that — because there is almost always something underneath.

You don't have to have it all sorted out before you talk. You don't have to explain it perfectly. You can just say *"I had a really big feeling and I don't totally understand it yet"* — and that is enough to start.

The big moment doesn't cancel you out. It's just part of the story.

And the story isn't over.